People of the Bible

The Bible through stories and pictures

Noah and His Ark

Copyright © in this format Belitha Press Ltd., 1982

Text copyright © Catherine Storr 1982

Illustrations copyright © Jim Russell 1982

Art Director: Treld Bicknell

First published in the United States of America 1982
by Raintree Publishers Inc.
330 East Kilbourn Avenue, Milwaukee, Wisconsin 53202
in association with Belitha Press Ltd., London.

Conceived, designed and produced by Belitha Press Ltd.,
2 Beresford Terrace, London N5 2DH

ISBN 0-8172-1975-7 (U.S.A.)

Library of Congress Cataloging in Publication Data

Storr, Catherine.
    Noah and his ark.

    (People of the Bible)
    Summary: A retelling of the story of the Flood that
lasted forty days, and the Ark on which Noah, his family,
and a pair of each kind of animal took refuge.

    1. Noah's ark—Juvenile literature. 2. Bible stories,
English—O.T. Genesis VI, 5-IX, 17. [I. Noah's ark.
2. Bible stories—O.T. Genesis] I. Russell, Jim, 1933-
ill. II. Title. III. Series.
BS658.S86   1982   222′.1109505   82-7712
    ISBN 0-8172-1975-7   AACR2

Printed in Hong Kong by South China Printing Co.

234567890   89 88 87 86 85

Noah and His Ark

RETOLD BY CATHERINE STORR
PICTURES BY JIM RUSSELL

Raintree Childrens Books
Milwaukee · Toronto · Melbourne · London
Belitha Press Limited · London

Once upon a time there lived a man called Noah. He had a wife and three sons— Shem, Ham, and Japheth. The sons had wives too.

One day, Noah heard God say to him,
"Noah! There is going to be a great flood,
and everyone in the world will be drowned.
You'll be the only people left alive.

"You must start at once to build a huge ship, with windows and doors. It must be big enough to hold you and your family and two of every kind of animal you can find."

Noah called his three sons, Shem, Ham, and Japheth. They went up the mountainside and cut down trees and sawed them into planks. They began to build the huge ship. They called it the Ark.

Noah's neighbors came and laughed at him. "What a stupid thing to do!" they said. "Why build a huge great ship like this, miles away from the sea?"

"Because there is going to be a great flood," Noah told them, but this only made them laugh more.

At last the Ark was finished. Noah and his sons and their wives went off to collect the animals. They found elephants, bears, zebras, cats, rabbits, mice, even spiders and ants.

Two of every kind came into the Ark, and were shown the stables, the cages, and the rooms where they were to live. The Ark was very crowded.

Just as the last tiny creature got inside,
the rain began.

At first his neighbors went on laughing.
"Just a shower!" they said.

But as the rain went on and the rivers rose
and the sea began to swell, they were
frightened.

First the water covered the roads and the fields. Then it came up to the windows of the houses. Then it came up to the roofs of the houses and the tops of the trees.

At last there was nothing to be seen in the whole world—except the Ark, sailing all alone in the world of water. And still it went on raining.

Noah told his family what to do. "Shem, you and your wife must feed all the animals. We have plenty of leaves and corn for the elephants and the rabbits. Ask the cow to give you milk for the cats. Don't let them eat the mice. Tell the bees to make honey for the bears."

"Ham," Noah said, "you and your wife must keep the animals clean. Sweep out the stables and wash the cages. Put all the dung into the special hole we made for it. We shall need it when the rain stops and we have to plant seeds in the earth."

"Japeth, you and your wife must collect
the rain water as it falls on the Ark,
so that we have fresh water to drink
and to wash with.

"Your mother is going to cook for all of
us, and I will help everyone with their work."

23

After forty long days and nights, the rain stopped. There was no dry land to be seen.

Noah sent out a raven to look for land. It did not come back, so Noah sent out a dove. But the dove could not find any land, and she came back to the Ark to rest.

A week later, Noah sent the dove out again, and that evening she came back with a leaf from an olive tree in her beak. Then Noah knew that the waters were sinking, and soon they would see dry land again.

After another seven days, Noah sent the dove out again. This time she did not come back at all, so he knew she had found some land where she could build her nest.

Soon afterward the Ark came to rest on dry land.

Noah opened the door of the Ark and
all the animals were very glad to come out.
Noah said to them, "Go off, stretch your
legs, eat all you can find, and have lots of
babies to fill this empty world."

Noah and his family were glad
to get out of the Ark. They began
to build houses and to make gardens
and to work in the fields again.

They wondered at first if there might be another flood, but God promised that this would never happen again.

To show that He remembered His promise, God put a rainbow in the sky.

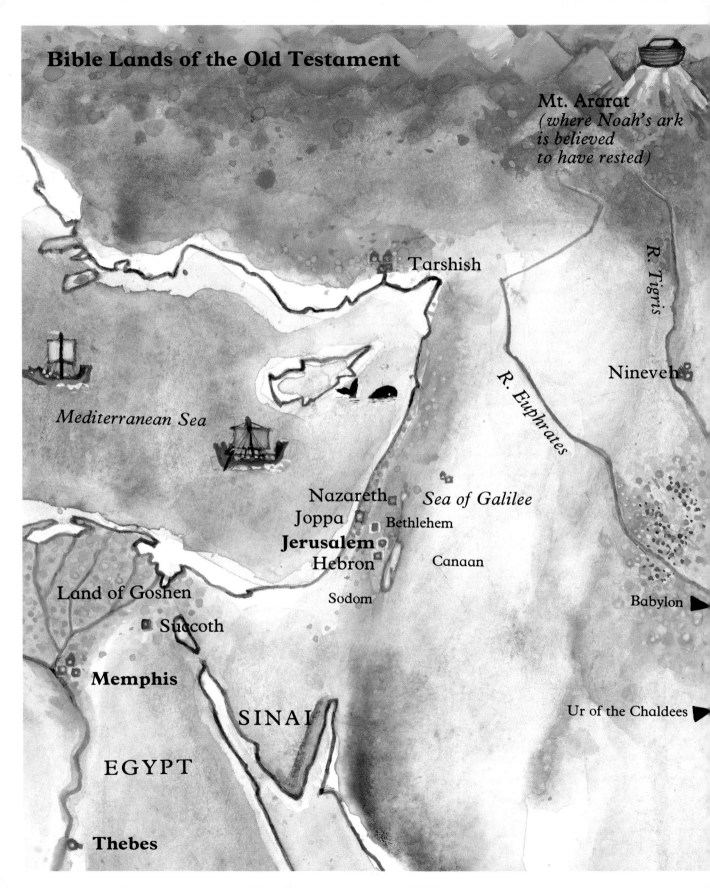

Bible Lands of the Old Testament

Mt. Ararat
*(where Noah's ark
is believed
to have rested)*

Tarshish

R. Tigris

Nineveh

Mediterranean Sea

R. Euphrates

Nazareth

Sea of Galilee

Joppa

Bethlehem

Jerusalem

Canaan

Hebron

Sodom

Babylon ▶

Land of Goshen

Succoth

Ur of the Chaldees ▶

Memphis

S I N A I

E G Y P T

Thebes